Untouched

A Poetry Collection

Ana Dee

Paperback: 978-1-7380546-0-2
eBook: 978-1-7380546-1-9
Hardcover: 978-1-7380546-2-6

Cover design by Leanne Booth

Grateful acknowledgements are made to the following publications in which some of these poems first appeared: *Sunday Mornings at the River, Campfire Poets, Small Leaf Press and Spillwords Press*

Duda, I miss you with every breath I take.

"August. We were arguing.
You want love to be like this every day don't you?
92 degrees even in the shade."

Jeanette Winterson, *Written on the Body*

Contents

Part I

Part II

Part V

Part VI

Part I

I yearn for summer lips and hands that are warm.
Do you have the power to revive a blue heart?
One that's been frozen over by too many winter storms.

Where You Are

I imagine myself
cold as ice
falling
into your
open arms.

Everyone says
it's beautiful
where I am
but I'd rather be
where you are.

In Stillness

I long for you
the way a blank canvas
yearns to be touched
by the hands of an artist,
which is to say
I long for you in stillness;
I long for you in silence.

Distance

Untouched lover,
even at a distance
you feel my ache.

I want.
I wonder.

I yearn.
I ache.

The Space Between Us

Pink –
like my lips calling out for you.

Fingers –
that are desperate to explore.

Close –
as I hate the space between us.

Whispers –
because nobody needs to know.

Of the Sea

In the morning when I wake,
my mouth tastes of the sea.

You must have swum miles
just to hold me in my dreams.

Grounded

We've been intimate
without touching.

For you, I'd shed my skin
and undress all my feelings.

You are the master
of my unravelling,
precious awakening.

Only you
keep me grounded
worlds apart.

This is Love

Scarlet skies
don't seem far
when the night is wine
and we're the stars.
Everything around us
screams this is love,
my love.

Unmapped

There are parts of the Earth
that remain unmapped –
unnamed glaciers and untamed peaks,
but I'd find it a shame
to leave you the same,
lying untouched and undiscovered
by my healing hands.

Tell me lover, would you let me
swim in your uncharted waters
and cross your secret bridge?
Could I venture and climb
the mountains of your mind
to uncover your hidden valleys
and ancient ruins?

I'd journey into the unknown
to turn your skin and bones into verse,
into psalm, into prayer, into art.
Could I be the first to name you,
to claim you, to declare you?

Love has turned me into an explorer,
desperate to save you.

Closer

Watch how the sky
bleeds for you –

how the sun idles
on your tender skin.

Its rays of light
are closer to your lips

than I've ever been.

Untouched

The sun sets and rises,
lavender skies melting
into specks of golden light
into pools of darkness.

A plane in the distance
leaves a trail I can't follow.
My thoughts start pulsing.
You are missing.

At night I walk in circles.
Dirty dishes pile up,
calls go unanswered.
All I do is think of you.

On one hand, I count
just enough reasons
to keep a steady mind
though I rarely feel at ease.

Inspiration plays games
of catch and release.
When it's my turn,
I write for hours.

You are my only muse.

Even in my sleep,
I am untouched.
Unbothered
by other bodies,

I only reach for you.

Love

When I think about you,

mind separates from body;
body separates from heart.

Straps separate from skin;
skin separates from blood.

All I am left with is love.

My Fears

My soft heart cradles
the darkest of thoughts.
They weigh on me heavy
but I don't make a sound.

Is my silence too silent?
Is my silence too loud?

Last night I stumbled out of a dream
where your arms were wrapped
tightly around my waist,
holding my wreckage together.

Have I said too much?
Have I not said enough?

The world has been cruel to me.
Only you have been good to me.

If I called for you in the middle of the night,
would you lie with me in the darkness?

Would you follow me into the mountains?
Would you help me bury my fears?

Wish

I wish I could stretch myself
across the ocean that divides us,

reach the coastline of your lips
and let the sweeping waves guide us.

I'd tell you *I've been waiting for you
my whole life, love.* Sink into me

where no one else can find us.

Sneaky Love

Sneaky little dove,
there's something wicked
about the way you love –
hiding your face when
creeping into my dreams
but always leaving tracks
so I know exactly where
those lips have been.

Out of Reach

I've been trying so hard
to get closer to you

but your heart is the moon:
hopelessly out of reach.

If You Weren't Afraid

A poem is where I go to drown [in you].

It's where I go to soar, to suffer,
to surrender, to scream; to lose myself
in all the beautiful things we could be.
I may be the poet, but you hold the pen,
you guide my fingers, you spin the keys.

I write for you to imagine
all the beautiful things we could be
if you embrace love without fear
of it decaying between your teeth.
If only you weren't so afraid of love.

If only you weren't afraid.

Masterpiece

Every time the fluorescent rain caresses my skin,
I think about the masterpiece we could create
from the wreckage that is me
and the storm that is you.

Turning Tides

He looks at me
as if I'm the flame
and he's the sea;

he'd turn his tide
for a chance
to burn with me.

Vision

And there you are:
A vision in the dark,
looking everything
and nothing

like love.

Part II

I want to hold you like it's the end
and love you like it's the beginning.

Electric Nights

You come to me like a spark of light
on my darkest night,
just when I thought I'd lost my way
and we have no time to waste,
so I'll tell you everything
you've been dying to hear.
Everything.
Because I want your everything.
I want your heart
when it abandons you,
to guide your hand
to inspire you,
never giving in to fear.
Come here.
If you hold my darkness close,
I'll share the weight of your grief
because when our souls collide,
I forget about the ones that came before:
the ghosts, the liars, the cheats.

These electric nights are made for lovers
and your hunger is made for me.

Your Eyes

Like tossed and scattered confetti,
all the stars fall to my feet
in sweet, sparkling surrender

and the moon is red with envy,
sensing I only have an appetite
for the light in your eyes.

My Lonely

I let my ghosts out for the night
so you can melt in my arms
like a delicate snowflake
falling onto the city street.

You've locked lips
with dozens of lovers
but you've never tasted
a loneliness this sweet.

Soul Deep

Crack me open
like the sun does the clouds
when she wants to break free.

I am writhing in vulnerability,
longing for a connection
that is more than just skin deep.

Like Everyone is Watching

My northern winds are screaming:
Love me like everyone is watching.

In the kitchen, a tea kettle whistling:
Leave traces every time we're touching.

Every light in the bedroom dancing
just to witness your cheeks blushing.

I wear your name on my hips all evening
and I feel nothing less than stunning.

Sacred Love

They told me to pick my poison
so I fell in love with you.

You're a creature of the dark.
I'm a creation of the dark.

We taste of the same grief,
the same love.

Speak to me in tongue.

I've never spoken to God,
but your name tastes holy in my mouth.

I'll hold you until I taste
God in my mouth.

I'll hold you until the scripts
of our souls become

our only religion.

Godly Woman

I always come to you in my Sunday best
expecting to be left undone.
You must be a man of God,
the way you make me believe in love.

Heavenly desire, kiss me
as if I stepped out of your wildest dreams.
If you wanted to, I'm certain you could
make a godly woman out of me.

Ghosts

I ache to see your dark side
and soft side.

Show me your raw side –
always, not only in the night time.

I'll take you on your worst day
on your worst side;

come to me with your broken side.

I'll hold the light while
you unveil your hidden side.

And if you have a haunted side
or a tendency to disappear after midnight,

I'll say *it's okay baby,*
come to me anyway.

I've been known to fall for ghosts.

Art

Eager are your eyes;
fragile is the night.

And the shell I wear is tight.

But if you're dying
to feel something,

lift the veil from my heart
and make *art* to me.

You can be the creator
and I'll be your creation.

My body will be the canvas
and your fingers, a paintbrush.

Show me you've got an eye for magic
in search for your next masterpiece

and for the final act of the night,
allow yourself to fall in *art* with me.

About Love

I don't know much about love

but I do know the way
my heart sings a familiar tune
when someone says your name
or how the mere sound of your voice
could answer all my prayers.

I know the world changes flavours
whenever you're around,
and how there's a swell of longing
wedged in the back of my throat –
and whenever I'm with you,

I lose all control.

A Taste of the Sun

after Nicholas Olah

There were tremors and swells in the sea –
warning signs – and grass-scented summer nights.
There were scenes out of dreams,
a stolen dance, a midnight romance,
curving roadways to nowhere and everywhere.
I took every right and every wrong
with a love whose hands changed
with the seasons.

There were lovers that caught my tongue
but barely caught my eye; lovers
who held their mouths wide open,
hoping for a taste of the sun (*it was never me*).
There were riverbeds and diamond rings,
confessions and apologies from dead-end flames
that only coloured me blue.
And then there was you.

And then there was you.

Moon

Wherever you go,
beautiful women
surround you like stars.
You can take your pick
when you have the face
and the body of a man
that makes women swoon.
But I am not a star.

I am the moon.

Midnight Eyes

I get so lost in
your midnight eyes
I forget my name,
the city we're in,
how we got here,
where we've been.

I'm oblivious to all
the secrets and sins.
It's hard to tell
where you end
and where I begin.

Part III

Rain over me.
I'll still set like the sun for you.

Lightning Snow

You longed for a soft summer love
so I gave you lightning snow.

Because what is love
if not creating something brand new?

What is love if not something electric,
something you're terrified to lose?

You must have known
I wasn't anything like the others;

all your sweet, surface-level lovers
have nothing in common with me.

Where they grow flowers,
I grow weeds.

Vanishing Acts

We commit vanishing acts
when things get too close.

We flirt like lovers
and love like ghosts.

About Me

If you ask them about me,

they'll say I devour lovers
the way the sea swallows the shore;
the way a slot machine swallows
a gambler's last two coins.
And that years after having a taste,
they can still feel my tongue lodged
in the hollows of their throats.

Perhaps in another world,
you could find someone better
(surely you could do much worse)
but the way you shiver
when we lock eyes tells me
you never knew real love,
and I must be your frightening first.

I bet you've never had a woman
touch you like this:

Right where it fucking hurts.

Your Moon

I want to be your moon
but I'm so afraid
of the s p a c e
between us.

Sweet Surrender

I don't want half of you,

I want all of you
to worship at my altar
and answer to the call of the night;

to surrender to me
the way Van Gogh
surrendered to his art.

Only then can I give you all of me.

My softest words,
my scarlet suffering,
my illusions of forever.

And a heartbreak to remember.

Hazards

Grasping for empty promises,
creating hazards
in the dark,
leaving a mess
we can't clean up
all in the name of love.

Silent and Still

The evening sun paints your skin gold.
I run my fingers down your sun-kissed face.

Time is not on our side, but tonight
your eyes are lightning pearls.

When they gaze at me,
I slither out of my shell

to hear our bodies roar like thunder
and exhale with the wind.

Hold tight

before the darkness drapes over us
like a blanket of melancholy

and I slip back into my skin
and you fall silent and still

all over again.

Quarter Moon

It doesn't matter
if you draw outside the lines
or colour me the darkest
shades of blue,
because what am I
but a quarter moon –
a piece of me
always missing
without you.

Midnight Blues

I've got the midnight blues
in the middle of the afternoon –
the side effects of missing you.

Beautifully Doomed

Desperate for answers,
I go searching in the stars.

I ask them:

On a scale of one to catastrophe,
how beautiful would they say we are?

Lighthouse

All aboard on your love ship.

I hear countless souls
have sailed before me
and none could endure
your tidal wave of emotions
before getting seasick.

Now I find myself like the others –
caught in your tumultuous storm,
restlessly fighting it from
trying to pull me overboard.

I'm starting to worry we'll sink
long before we reach the shore;
long before I show you
I may be the lighthouse
you've spent your whole life searching for.

Alert

You are the thunderstorm warning
and I'm dancing in acid rain.

Overflowing

If love is rain,
ours is always pouring
without warning.

We are passion-soaked beings,
emotions overflowing.

Old Flames

We kiss like fire and wind,
drifting into the woods
of our unspoken sins.

Whispers

Love me in whispers.

Nobody needs to know
I'm in your blood.

Nobody needs to know
you're in my bones.

Selfish

I cross the line for illicit love
with a touch softer than cotton.

If loving you is selfish,
I choose to be spoiled rotten.

No Entry

You want to taste my ruby lips
but fear they'll leave a mark.

Loving you is trespassing:

Forbidden access
to an insecure heart.

Dark

I like myself better in the dark.

I'm less of a monster
and more of a lover
when the lights are off.

Maybe in the dark,
you could see me
for who I really am.

Maybe in the dark,
I could become
someone you love.

Lovers Anonymous

Do lovers hold hands?
Do they keep secrets?
Do they do what you do to me?

Love when it's convenient.

Empty Dreams

Rebellious and charming.
You captured my heart
from the very beginning

but since then,
it's been nothing
but loose ends.

Empty promises,
empty dreams.
Empty lives.

Empty me.

Secrets

Are we running out of love
or out of time?

I can't keep hiding
behind moonlit secrets
buried between mountains
you'll never climb.

Dust

We've become immersed in dreams
drawn out of dust.

We're losing our way
and when echoes of love fade

I'm afraid nothing will be left of us.

Muse

If you can't be my lover,
be my midnight muse;
my midnight blues.
Be my worst-kept secret,
my open, oozing wound.

I'm not afraid to speak about
all the ways you've cut me open;
to put this longing on display
in front of everyone I know and say:
Watch how beautifully I ache for you.
How I come apart for you.

This ink is tired of spilling its blood for you
but there is no other way.
I spend all of my days
writing to feel closer to you
and only feel closer to myself.
I speak to you in the language of memory
and beckon you like it's my dying breath.

Thunder Love

Thunder lover,
you took this heart by storm.

Now I'm always looking
for love in the rain.

Choices

In life we're given choices.
You've always been mine.

Now love is standing
in the other room

waiting for you to decide.

Beginnings and Endings

after Nicholas Olah

When they ask what the beginning felt like

Say a stab of hope.
Crystal waterfalls.
Hidden treasures.
The backseat of a lover's car.
Say cookie-sized confetti.
A secret language.
A soul taking flight.
Two hearts racing.

A love that has no time for waiting.

When they ask what the ending felt like

Say an endless darkness.
Stuttered breaths.
A shipwreck.
Say a stolen future.
An ache you didn't know existed.
Ghost towns.
Empty liquor bottles.
A mouthful of lies.

A love that's run out of time.

Part IV

Love is a compass
pointing you in my direction
while you follow the wrong one home.

The Art of Our Tongue

How could you even think
to speak to her in our words?

To breathe her in
with my lungs?

Nobody understands you because
I'm the only language you speak.

You're only fluent
in the art of our tongue.

Another World

In another world,
I don't have to question

where you've been
or who you've become

because you are the promising blue sky
and I, your morning sun.

I only rise for you,
and you always wait for me.

In another world, we are timeless
and what we have is enough.

You don't cut corners;
there are no shortcuts to love.

You only come home to me.

Thief

Loving you is returning to the scene of a crime
and all I want to do is confess.

Take a drop of my blood.
Ink my fingerprints.

Tell the whole world
it was me.

I wanted to be more than your lover,
more than your other.
But instead I became a thief.

Just Love

Love is just love

until you start licking blood
off the fingers that are tearing
through your floorboards.

It's just love until
you open your mouth to speak
and end up spilling like a river at his feet.

Love is just love
until an ache settles between your ribs
and you call it by his name.

Ghost Stories

My favourite ghost story
is the one where you don't go quietly.
I want the writing on the wall.
If this isn't it,
I need to hear you
scream it to me loud.
The worst thing you could do
is disappear without a trace,
without a reason,
without a goodbye.

My favourite ghost story
is the one where you don't go at all.
But if you must,
then leave blood,
leave wounds,
leave scars.
Leave *something*,
so when they ask about
my haunted heart,
I can say *it may look empty now,*
but my body is proof
that love lived here once.

Starless Night

You were every bit of heaven
if heaven were real –

radiating light, strong enough
to make a broken woman heal.

Without you, I'm a starless night;
a hollow heart that doesn't feel.

Now watching you vanish
makes me question:

Were you ever even real?

My Demise

I should have stopped
to read the signs:

B e w a r e
of his wildfire eyes.

Now the embers
that I'm left with

will be my demise.

Small Town Sins

You were haunted when I met you.

You were burdened, you were in pain
from carrying the weight of your father's guilt
and your mother's shame and there was nothing
I could do to make it go away because

I was haunted before we met.

But I still loved you like I was on fire
because I, too, grew up in a house of flames.

We wore matching wounds,
burned from the same rage
and smelled of small town sins –
suffocating secrets
that could outright kill a man.

Untold

How do I write our end
when we've hardly even begun?

Our story remains untold.
My demons, you've left untamed.

And they only answer
to your name.

Close

We were so close,

I could taste your tortured soul;
you could soak up my infinite grief.
Oceans apart, I carried your name
on the roof of my mouth;
placed your stories for safekeeping
underneath my tongue.
We were so close,
you carved out a space for my pain
in between your palms and buried
my secrets deep inside your lungs.

I've never known of anything more intimate
than an untouched love.

Now we lie awake
beside foreign bodies,
our stolen bodies
tending to our lonely
beneath a collapsing sky.
Forgive me if this is too much,
too soon, too loud...
I just can't help thinking
about how we were close,
so close, ever so close.

Sea of You

All my friends
are begging me
to pull through

but I can't –
for I am still lost
in the sea of you.

For You

I'd abandon my flesh and my bones
if it means I could take you home again.

I'd turn myself inside out,
outside in, whichever you prefer.

Trust in me to fulfill your desires;
your every wish will be my command.

So tell me how you want to be touched,
how you want to be loved,
how you want to be held.

I've always cared for you
better than I've ever cared
for myself.

Skyline

Honey,
my hungry heart aches
for another taste
of the magic you used to pour.

Many would move mountains for you
but my only desire is to reach
the skyline of your soul.

Little Lies

And so he says:

Cheer up baby,
in a few months' time,
you won't even remember
what your lips felt like on mine.

Colours

I used every colour on my palette
to bring you back to life.

Now you paint the most
beautiful rainbows

in someone else's sky.

The Absence of You

The absence of you has a rhythm,
a voice, a pulse,
a scent.

I can't help that my soul remembers
all the things my skin forgets.

Every night I write
just so I can taste you again.

If not with my lips,
then with my pen.

Tomorrow I'll take a train to visit
all the places we've never been.

I search for you in words,
in verses, in spaces,
in sins.

Beautiful Truths

I want to write the most beautiful truths
for you to fall into my arms again.

This winter is exceptionally cruel.
The words – they just don't come.

So I do what I can:
I water the plants, bake the bread,

fold the laundry, drink tea
instead of coffee.

My fingers hover over the typewriter keys
for hours at a time but the words –

they still don't come.

I smell of cinnamon and sorrow;
only wind gusts tap on my window.

I swear I'm trying everything
to survive these heavy winter nights.

I want to write you the most beautiful poetry
but the words don't come.

And neither does the sun.

Clockwork Heart

My clockwork heart
is a ticking time bomb.

I'd rip it from my chest
just to taste the flesh.

I imagine it tastes
a lot like you.

Ellipsis

Like a parched land
that thirsts for the rain's touch,
I want to catch every word
that pours from your mouth.

Remember, our midnight tongues
on the cusp of surrender
with our unspoken truth
and you: my unfinished verse.

If you choose me now,
I'll come to you like a time capsule
and love you in reverse
because you are my muted desire;
a seed of possibility.

You are the pause
that stretches into eternity.

Let the moon be my witness:
You are my ellipsis.

Remember Me

Silent suffering, you kill me
with your brilliant forgetting.
I just can't accept that you've already
wiped me from memory,
when you've always held me
like I was something never-ending;
something life-changing,
something absolute.
For as long as I've known you,
you've been running from the truth.
Do I always need to beg you for the truth?

Tonight I'm begging you to crawl
between my lines and spaces,
recreate the nights
where you'd unearth my magic
and ink my pages –
leave a sign that you remember me.
Let me sink into your chest to hear
the quickening of your breath
while I whisper:

Remember me,
remember me,
remember me.

The Beginning

I loved you
like you were the tender night sky
and I, your midnight moon;
like we were written in the stars.

I loved you
like you were the valley of life
and I, your restless river.
A priceless work of art.

And I still love you.
It's like you're the author of my madness
and I'm a blank page, waiting to be inked.

Write my ending –
but spare my heart,
while I dream of the beginning.

Part V

They told me you're a creation
of the same grief I hold in my mouth.

Emergency

Ever since you left

I've been a wicked nightmare,
a vicious wreck,
a haunted refuge –
a home for angry men.

Honey, I've let all the bad guys in.

My sinister sin, I'm afraid
there's no goodness in me left.
I've become an ancient curse
trapped inside a godless church

where there's no room for salvation
or my deepest temptations
when I'm a stranger to myself.
I've become so angry

and tonight I'm on fire.

Tired of being a liar, I call
to confess I need you hopelessly.
Endlessly. Desperately.
Consider it an emergency.

I am the emergency.

Tulip

We take the train
into the tainted town
we once called home.
My petals have been
picked since the last
time we spoke, so
touch me gently and
love me tenderly
when we're

a

l

o

n

e.

I'm your twisted,
tarnished tulip
blowing steadily
in the w i n d,
already thinking
of all the ways
I can slip through
your fingers

a

g

a

i

n.

Unwrap Me

Delicate disaster,
you've always known how
to leave me achingly undone

so unwrap me with a memory –

one I can sink my teeth into,
whose heat will make me shiver
like a snow-kissed winter's sun.

Wounds

Darling,
you and I both know
some things are better left unsaid;
some wounds are better left untouched.
But there are so many things
that still tear me apart
and you are present
in every single one.
For the sake of our sanity,
I don't tell you how much;
instead, I let my heart bleed
into notebooks and pens
as the flame between us
fights for its final breath.
And though there are days
when I wake with the weight
of acceptance, knowing
you won't be mine again,
most days I still struggle
to separate my soul from yours.

Darling, oh darling,
I'm simply dying to know:
Is this a wound I carry alone?

Out of Sight

I buried my love for you
behind the moon
and blamed it on the stars;
cursed the day we met
and wrote you away in the sky.

I thought I could escape the truth
if it was out of sight
but every time I'm out for blood,
starving and searching
for a stranger to love,
I come back empty.

Desperately hungry for you.

Unholy Gods

In my darkest hours,

I dwell over how I lost you
to the hunger of the night;

how another body trespassed
so effortlessly over our temple

and burned our safe haven
to the ground.

Unholy gods tend to my wounds
and kiss my scars,

but none could ever live up
to what you were, or what you are.

When I hold my breath underwater,
it's you that fills my lungs.

I feed on the flesh of faceless lovers
and ache for you in a forbidden tongue.

Something Holy

A man is just a man
until he becomes a god in your arms.
A sanctuary for your ill-fitted skin.

When he calls himself a man of faith,
you peel off your insecurities like sins
and leave them buried in the pockets
of his collarbones.

That's when his body becomes
the only place of worship you know –
the only one you could ever devote yourself to.

Years will pass by before you realize
man is not god and love is not religion.
And who can you blame for being so wrong?

This is what happens
when you keep mistaking love
as something holy.

Beautiful Together

Come fire, come water;
you still burn in me, long lost lover.

Could last night's dream be a sign?

You left your soul prints
on the curves of my thighs.

Come winter, come summer;
you still linger in me, reckless lover.

You've made a wreck out of me
like a natural disaster, but in my dreams

you collect all the rubble to light us a fire.
And we look beautiful, burning together.

We could have been beautiful together.
We could have been burning together.

Another You

What if I told you
I found another you?

He speaks to me in love –
a language I don't understand

because I only know our tongue.
I only know your tongue.

Haunting Hunger

A new moon;
an old, hollow ache.
His lips on mine –
an intruding taste.
Though I find comfort
in his late nights
and the warmth of his chest,
something inside me brews:
A haunting hunger
coated with your name.

The night closes in on me.

Memories of love lost
flood my dismal mind.
To stay afloat,
I use his heart
as a crutch.
But when his lips
depart my skin,
the ache remains,
untouched.

You

Does it bother you that I prefer you?

That if I could have anyone in the world,
I would still choose you?

You've taken over my mind
but someone else takes off my clothes.

I close my eyes when he touches me
and his hands become yours.

When he speaks, his voice is a distant memory
and his lips turn into yours.

He has good reason to fear losing me.
I've given him every reason to let go.

He's always been afraid
to let me out of his arms

lest I fall back into yours.

Mirror, Mirror

Reflective stranger,
you dream of euphoria
so you've been reaching
but never latching on.

You stare back at me –
wild eyes, velvet lips,
dressed in my desires,
ready for a night of sin.

If I were him, I must admit,
I wouldn't let you in.

Inconsistent Consistencies

I come to him in waves with my love,
all chaotic and cluttered
from being hung up and twisted
in strands of love for another.

Our hearts are intertwined
in knots that can't be undone
and for him I can't say the same,
so I only come in waves.

Some days I manifest a storm
and others, barely a breeze –
but never something constant;
never something in between.

Tonight I come in waves
barely touching the shore
and if my sea ever decides to settle,
will it be too little, too late?

How long will I wander?
How long will he wait?

Desert

He holds me like I'm holy
and consumes every liquid lie
that seeps out of my filthy mouth.

As if I'm the reason he's alive,
he'd swallow every single drop of me
like he's been caught in the deepest of droughts.

There's no need for him to tell me he loves me.
I'm a frequent patron of this forsaken desert;
I've already figured him out.

Yours

Last night he asked for forever
as he wrapped his hands around my waist
but then the moon caught my eye
and I pictured you in his place.
And it's not just me,
because when I looked up
even the stars spelled out:

Yours,
even when I'm someone else's.

Now all I can think about is how
he'll watch me walk down the aisle,
thinking he'll become the happiest man
alive, but then the wind will howl:

Yours,
even when I'm someone else's.

He could promise me the world
and it still won't matter when
the wind whispers through the trees
carrying your name in the breeze,
it's as if the universe seeks
to remind me

I'm still yours –
even when I'm someone else's.

Unwelcome

I wish I could bury you with my words
and write you out of existence
(and even if I could, I know it wouldn't last long)
because I can still feel you
in the sweat between his palms
and I can only taste you
when his lips wake me at dawn.

Must you always fucking linger
in places you don't belong?

Lightning Love

Lightning lover,

I wonder if you know
you're the reason why

I'm always chasing the storm.

Senses

The thought of you
awakens all my senses.
My soul whispers *remember*.
My mind insists I forget.

Every night I'm at war with myself.

Though it may seem like
I've put our past behind me,
I'm afraid I'll never feel that spark
with anyone else –

not ever, not ever, not ever
because darling, I still burn for you.
And if you were to come knocking on my door,
I'd fall right to my knees and tell you

I surrender,
I surrender,
I surrender.

Behind Closed Doors

For what it's worth,

I still call for you in breathless whispers
and ache for you in suppressed moans.

When I'm finished with you,
I tuck you in between the pages of my books

the same way I used to hold you
behind closed doors.

I don't speak about the time I was a thief
coming home with empty pockets,

stepping into a room
void of soul, void of light.

A thief who tiptoed past the truth
so she could sleep at night.

Tell me darling,
can you sleep at night?

'Cause I still can't sleep at night.

The Truth

You live in the blank spaces
between my words;
the hushed breaths
between my cries.

You are the truth
and I'm so afraid
to set you
free.

Realizations

I've been holding on so tightly
to the remains of our love,
it's been suffocating me.

No, you never took my breath away.
You took the life out of me.

Our Undoing

When they ask about our undoing,
say it wasn't our time.

We were two lonely strangers
aching and desperate for love.

Say I couldn't answer your heart;
you couldn't speak to my soul.

We were a match made in hell
and we burned in our ruins.

Admit you found someone else
who's twice as much as I ever was

but only half as good.

Part VI

*I'm no longer your damsel in distress,
your twisted tulip, your tender rose.*

*I have a language of my own now
and it's not yours.*

Bruised Fruit

Like tender fruit,
I spoil in the wrong hands.

One moment I'm sweet,
the next I'll be so bitter,
so cruel, so silently loud
but don't get it twisted:
I'll still be the best thing
you've ever held in your mouth.

My heart is an overripe peach
desperate to be picked,
to be touched, to be loved.
Press into my flesh –
I'm bound to stick to your skin
like a childhood scar.

I'll be the uninvited lingering mess,
dripping down your hands.

*All I want is to be held through the night
without leaving blood on anyone's hands.*

Self-Love

I am still learning to love
all the parts of me
you kept hidden.

Words

Words have taken hostage of my tongue.

All the things I'm too afraid to say
collect like volcanic ash in my lungs.

Vulnerabilities bleed on paper
but leave my mouth
never.

What You've Made of Me

I am what you've made of me:
majestic skies and open seas,
inked pages and typewriter keys;
midnights charged with memories.

I've become the hungry skyline
blessing these dark cities,
alternate endings and mysteries;
bruised fruit falling tenderly.

I am what you've made of me:
the devastating last words
you said to me.

But don't I wear them beautifully?

Waterfall Woman

Rivers of love flow through my veins.

Sometimes, it's too much to contain
this overwhelming need to spill.

I need to share.
I need to save.
I need to give.

Maybe it's because
I am a waterfall of a woman.

It's no wonder why
I'm always ready to spill.

Room With a View

Before you begin to remember

the ocean breeze,
the lemon tree,
the moonlight bursting
through our window
desperate for a peek,
my powder white dress,
the way we used to breathe...

Close your eyes and tell yourself
it was nothing but a fever dream.

Flavour of Forever

There is nothing gentle
about red lips,
soft skin,
frosted lace
over porcelain bones,
lucid dreams
that leave you
dripping –
starving
for a flavour of forever.
These are dangerous desires
and nothing more.

Fiercely Feminine

I am red velvet.

Love bites. Hand prints.
The sparkle in the stars.
The tears in your eyes.

I am strawberry fields.

Sweet wine. July sunsets.
Naked words. Cherry trees.
Lush gardens. Ocean waves.

Baby, I am
every phase
of the moon.

I am heat. I am citrus
dripping down
your chin.

Fiercely feminine,
I am the revolution.
The divine.

I am my own fucking god.

Fairytales

I could blind hearts with my starlight eyes
and rebrand skin with velvet-coated lies.

Everyone chases fairytales and magic
until love becomes an illusion.

That Witch

I'm the witch your mother warned you about.

The seductive sorceress
that'll devour you in the dark.

It's true what they say about me:
I'd summon all the spirits just to feel your love

because I'm your raging tempest;
your gateway and obstacle to heaven.

I don't even need to cast a spell on you
to be worshipped like a religion.

What I'll Become

I am tropics. I am storm.
I am less body than I am soul.
I am borderless.

I am life-changing words.
Sunsets on the horizon.
I am the things I hold onto tightest.

I am the heaviness in my chest.
Poetry in motion.
I am a whisper of what I used to be

and an echo of what I'll become.

Something Different

You are becoming something different:

Yellow cherry blossoms.
Midnight sun.
Full body breaths.
Exotic language.
A fifth season
in full bloom.
Glowing skin.
Dew-soaked toes.

And that beautiful mouth.
That sanctuary tongue.

You show me the places
love touches you

that I didn't know were there.

How I Love

Soul stripped.
Heart unguarded.
Stepping
  over
    the edge.
On the tips
of my toes.
Arms outstretched,
reaching.
Wide eyes, feet bare
s o a r i n g.
Back to the wind.
Face to the sun.
This is how I live.
This is how I love.

The Unspoken

I haven't forgotten about you.

You live in the breaths
I can barely take,

the poetry I cannot
bring myself to write.

You live in the unspoken,
the untouched;

places I don't dare visit,
don't dare touch.

Beautiful Sins

I fall into the softest embrace of the night
and I write and I write and I write.
I write like no one's reading;
I write to keep our love alive.

When I've written our story,
I'll fling open the curtains,
unlock my heart's doors,
let all prospective lovers
like the sun stream in,

and I'll name all my
beautiful sins
after you.

Purple Prayers

I found it odd from the start –
the way you never stop to stare at art
or the way you sleepwalk through life
untouched by all the things
that make me feel alive.
You don't weep to songs in the dark
or sing when life gets hard.
You pass by museums
as if they're not worthy of your eyes –
am I?
You have no time for books
and poetry is strange to you;
these conversations
are a little too intense for you, I know.
You said art never made sense,
so it's no wonder why my words
don't make sense to you.
My mind you find unruly.
My poetry, unholy.
My shades of blue, ghastly.

Now I wonder
if I were to paint my lips red
and shed my shades of blue,
would it turn my words
into the purest purple prayers
or would that still be
too much blue for you?

If I buried my soul with the night
and undressed myself
of other people's pain,
would that change
your mind about me?
If I became drop-dead red
(redder than a traffic light;
redder than the blood
pumping through your veins)
would it drive you a little insane?
Would you wear me with pride
on your heart?

I could be a bleeding masterpiece
and you still wouldn't *see* me.

You never stop to stare at art.

Sea of Love

I set sail eagerly
and hungrily
on the sea of love,
to which there is
no end in sight –

only bright beginnings.

Acknowledgements

Special thanks to Nicholas Olah whose two poems served as the foundation for my own creations in "A Taste of the Sun" and "Beginnings and Endings," crafted as after poems to his beautiful work. Grateful acknowledgements also go to Maria Giesbrecht for her exceptional prompts that sparked the creation of my poems "Ghost Stories," "Small Town Sins," and "Purple Prayers."

I would also like to credit the movies that provided the initial and closing lines of two poems: the first line of "You" finds its origins in the film "La Carrière de Suzanne" while the final line of "We Were So Close" draws from the film "Paris, je t'aime."

My heartfelt thanks go to each reader who picked up this book and delved into its pages, making my greatest dream come true. Without you, these words would only exist inside my head.

Author Profile

Ana Dee (Đermanović) is a confessional poet and old school
soul currently based in Ontario, Canada, originally from Serbia.
Her poetry has most recently appeared in *Spillwords Press (Summer
2023) Sunday Mornings at the River Poetry Anthology (Fall 2022),
Campfire Poets (Campfire One, Fall 2022), Small Leaf Press (Summer
2022), and Train River Poetry anthology (Winter 2020).*

When she's not weaving her poetic magic, she can be found
unleashing her vocal prowess at karaoke, finding solace in nature
and daydreaming about a less complicated existence by the ocean.

Untouched is her highly anticipated debut poetry collection.

Connect with her on Instagram for new poems and writing updates.
@anadeewrites